William J. Cherry

**A Hand-Book of the City of Rock Hill**

William J. Cherry

**A Hand-Book of the City of Rock Hill**

ISBN/EAN: 9783337328450

Printed in Europe, USA, Canada, Australia, Japan

Cover: Foto ©Lupo / pixelio.de

More available books at **www.hansebooks.com**

# A HAND-BOOK

OF THE

# CITY OF ROCK HILL

CONTAINING

A Brief Summary of Her Past; Some Facts

and Figures about Her Present, with

a Glance at Her Prospects

for the Future.

———

## "THE HUB OF THE PIEDMONT"

———

A Lively Little City of Upper South Carolina.

1895.

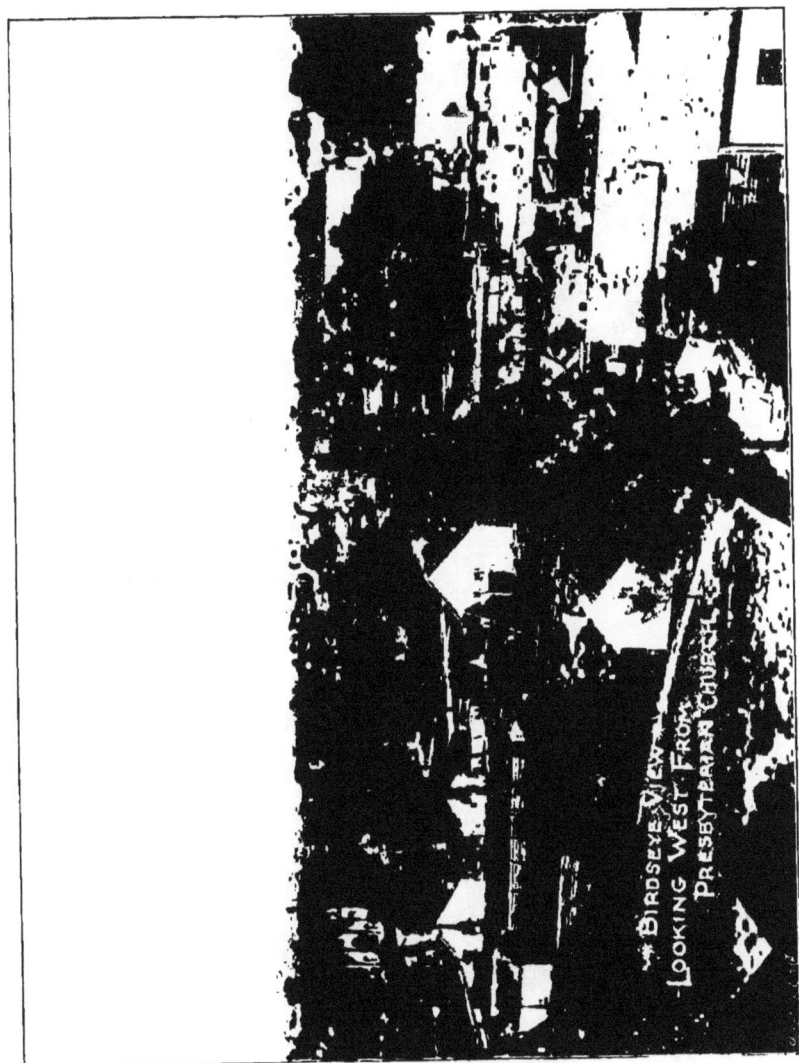

BIRDSEYE VIEW

—LOOKING WEST FROM

PRESBYTERIAN CHURCH.

# PREFATORY

Life is too short and time too long for engaging in wordy explanations. This manual is not intended for an advertisement, though such should become one of its incidents. It is written because there is something to write about which stirs the heart of every citizen of Rock Hill with pardonable pride, and because of the desire to permanently record facts and figures which tell of an enterprising and progressive people, and which will act as a stimulus for the future. It is synoptical and summary. Finally, it is written from a standpoint of Truth; and, while it is desired to present its subject matter in as neat a garb as possible, nothing will be stated which cannot be readily verified.

# To Hon. William C. Hutchison,

## MAYOR OF THE CITY OF ROCK HILL.

My Dear Sir :

This little sketch is dedicated to you, as a tribute to your public-spirited liberality; in acknowledgment of your generous assistance in bringing this work to a successful issue ; and as an expression of personal esteem and friendship.

WILLIAM J. CHERRY.

October, 1895.

SAINT PERA
S. LUCIANUS

THE RODDEY BUILDING

# Rock Hill and Vicinity.

• •

The wonderful story of Rock Hill's progress has many times been attempted, but all of the truth about this wide-awake, thrifty and progressive little city has never been told. The limited compass of this sketch forbids the writer to do more than touch upon salient features. Passing undaunted through the thick darkness of financial distress that settled as a pall over all this country for the last few years, Rock Hill turns now to the promises of the morning and greets with joy the gray streak which betokens the coming sunshine of a cloudless day. She is prepared to make good her claim that she is the ideal city of South Carolina. Situated among the foot-hills and fertile valleys of upper Carolina, in the great Piedmont Belt; with a climate that is salubrious in summer and bracing in winter; with water that is pure freestone, limpid and cold; with good health, good schools and elegant church edifices; with macadamized streets, sidewalks paved with granite, street cars, electric lights, and all of the other conveniences of a first-class modern town; with her industries and enterprises, wonderful in their number and variety for a city so young; with her highly favored location in the midst of a productive farming section, owned by an intelligent and prosperous agricultural class; and, not the least of all, with a population of cultured, refined, home loving and hospitable people, ever ready to bid the visitor and the stranger welcome; with all of these attractions and numerous others which need not be particularized, she stands squarely in the lead among her sister cities and towns of the State, and presents claims to all who are seeking an ideal home which are scarcely equalled and not excelled.

# Ibistorical and Municipal.

Rock Hill's natal star twinkled into sight in the year 1870, the town then becoming a corporate existence. Its first executive head consisted of the following officers: John R. Allen, Intendant; J. M. Ivy, Dr. T. L. Johnson, M. W. Russell and John Ratterree, Wardens. The last named warden is the only member of the original town council now living.

The original charter was a crude and simple affair, and was soon found inadequate to the demands of a thriving and growing town. It was amended and enlarged by the State Legislature from time to time to meet the exigencies of the changing conditions. It became thus of a fragmentary and patch-work character, and was not long to be tolerated in this condition. In the year 1892, the young town, having grown into a stalwart municipality of several thousand souls, decided to put aside the ways of childhood and to apply for sisterhood into the galaxy of South Carolina cities. So that, in December of that year, the Legislature of the State granted to Rock Hill a full and complete city charter, conferring the most liberal and ample governmental privileges, powers and functions, and changing the name of the corporation to that of "The City of Rock Hill."

The first City Council elected under the City Charter was composed of the following persons: Dr. John W. Fewell, Mayor; Ed. E. Poag, Edward R. Avery, A. J. Thompson, John J. Waters, W. J. Irby and W. H. Wylie, Aldermen.

The present City Council is composed of W. C. Hutchison, Mayor; W. G. Reid, John J. Waters, R. Lee Kerr, E. R. Avery, L. M. Davis and J. A. Green, Aldermen.

The Police Department is at present officered as follows: F. W. Culp, Chief; J. F. Doby, L. D. Wilkinson, A. L. Wallace and J. M. Devinney, Assistants.

These gentlemen who administer the affairs of the city government

6

are young men of sterling business qualities, who are always alive to the interests of the corporation.

The sanitary laws of the State affecting cities and incorporated towns are rigidly enforced, and the following efficient Board of Health is in charge of the Health Department: Dr. W. J. White, President; Dr. T. L. Cornwell, Health Officer; W. A. Fewell, Secretary and Treasurer; the other members being T. L. Johnson and W. L. Hall.

Rock Hill has always been fortunate in having good men at the head of public affairs, and this has been an important factor in her progress. In politics, as in everything else affecting the city's welfare, the people have never been divided, and in all elections, it is merely a choice between men and the selecting of the best men for office.

But affairs of local government have not absorbed the attention of the citizen of Rock Hill, and a few facts will serve to show that he has been active along other lines. Could the men who christened "Rock Hill" when an infant cross-roads village a few years ago, have foreseen the Rock Hill of to-day, they might have thought the name too insignificant.

## NAME.

The little incident to which this city owes its name will probably not be devoid of interest. About the time the Charlotte and South Carolina Railway had been completed through this section, in or near the year 1852, a party of gentlemen, residing in the vicinity of the station to be here located, had met and were discussing the matter of a name. There was at that time an immense quantity of flint rock imbedded on the hill which is the present site of Mr. John Ratterree's residence. The hint was caught from this circumstance; some one of the party proposed that the station be called "Rock Hill," and the name was adopted.

The name is an illustration of the philosophy of 'that which we call a rose by another name.' A name is only valuable for what it represents, and Rock Hill stands for all that is set down on these pages, and more. It is the name by which an enterprising corporation has become known—a name now much used on all sides—and no Rock Hillian could be induced to give it up. It is his talisman.

## LOCATION.

Rock Hill is situated in the northern part of the State of South Carolina, in York County; eighty-four miles from Columbia, and twenty-five miles from Charlotte, N. C., with which points it is connected by rail. The city stands 668 feet above tide water, and is the highest point on the Charlotte, Columbia and Augusta Railroad between Augusta and Charlotte It possesses excellent advantages in its railroad facilities; the Charlotte, Columbia and Augusta, and Ohio River and Charleston Railroads intersecting in the heart of the city. The great Seaboard System is discussing the project of connecting with Rock Hill by the Georgia, Carolina and Northern, and no doubt such a connection will be effected at no distant day. This last named road, extending from Atlanta, Ga.. to Portsmouth, Va., is already near enough to materially affect freight rates and to become an important connection for travelling.

Here is what was said of Rock Hill's advantages of location by a disinterested writer seven years ago: "With direct communication north, east, south and west, contiguous to inexhaustable timber and mineral wealth, and located in the heart of a farming country capable of growing the greatest diversity of crops known in any one climate, this favored town offers all that could be desired for manufacturing purposes. Already, independent of all other considerations, only a little time is asked to make it a great distributing point."

## RAPID PROGRESS.

Captain W. L. Roddey, one of Rock Hill's leading citizens, is the owner of the first plat of the territory which is the present site of Rock Hill. This original plat is neatly framed and well preserved, and is an interesting relic. It was made in November, 1851, by Deputy Surveyor John Roddey, father of Captain Roddey, and was in anticipation of the

coming of the Charlotte and South Carolina Railroad, which had been previously projected. It provided for twenty-three lots along what is now Main Street, the whole of the district then surveyed being a woodland where birds chattered and built their nests unmolested.

When the Charlotte and South Carolina (now the Charlotte, Columbia and Augusta) Railroad was completed through this section, in 1852, not a single business house marked the present site of Rock Hill. Up to 1870 Rock Hill amounted to only an insignificant village, with the advantage of a railroad station and other slight conveniences. When incorporated in 1870, its population was 273; in 1880, its population had increased to 809; at the end of the next decade it had reached 2,781; and in 1891, by the town census, it was 3,804. The assessed valuation of property for taxation in 1887 was $451,119; in 1890 it was $959,401 ; in 1891 it was $1,222,276, an increase of over 171 per cent. in four years.

### ROCK HILL OF TO-DAY.

The present population of Rock Hill is 5,500; the present taxable value of Rock Hill property is $1,255,460; her yearly business amounts to $3,500,000 ; she handles annually, on an average, 18,000 bales of cotton ; she has in operation three cotton factories (spinning and weaving) representing a capital of $435.000.00, and two more in process of erection, which will employ a capital of $325,000.00, aggregating in cotton manufacturing, a capital of $760,000.00; a buggy, carriage and wagon factory, with authorized capital of $75,000.00; a tobacco factory with an authorized capital of $40,000.00; a door, sash and blind factory; a canning factory; an electric light plant, with arc and incandescent lights; a town site company; a street railway and water works company; machine shops, etc.

The weekly pay-roll from Rock Hill's manufactories amounts to more than $6,000.

# Minerals.

Mining in this section has received little attention; but to this wonderful story of growth and prosperity a new phase will be added when the mineral wealth of this section is begun to be developed. Immense quantities of iron ore are imbedded in the earth in this vicinity, containing not a trace of sulphur or phosphorus, and assaying 62 to 69 per cent. of magnetic iron; and nine miles away, near the Ohio River and Charleston Railroad, are large deposits of hematite ore in fine condition for smelting, which yields 60 per cent. of magnetic iron.

There are several gold mines in the neighborhood, which have, at various times, been worked, the ore from two extensive veins near here yielding from $16 to $350 per ton.

When it is considered that our increasing railroad facilities will before long bring the coal fields of Tennessee to our doors, it will thus be seen that the mineral wealth of this section is not to be discounted as a factor in making of Rock Hill a great city.

● ●

# Financial.

Rock Hill has a banking and loaning capital of $400,000.00; divided between the First National Bank, the Savings Bank, the Rock Hill Real Estate and Loan Company, the Southern Loan and Investment Company and the Mutual Home Building and Loan Association.

### BANKING.

Every live town and every prosperous business community must have good banking facilities, and this important fact was not to escape the foresight of Rock Hill's sagacious business men. Hence we find two banks springing into existence almost simultaneously in 1886-87. There were private banking concerns prior to that time, but it was felt that the time for more extended operations along this line had come.

The banks and the people are interdependent, and it would be difficult to conceive how one could get along without the other. The Rock Hill banks have always had the fullest confidence of those having business relations with them; and the remembrance of many favors bestowed by the banks, gives them a place in the hearts of the people of this city and community.

Not a breath of suspicion has ever tarnished the fair fame of Rock Hill's banks; and they have passed unscathed and without a shadow of alarm through the late financial panic which swept over the country. This fact alone is abundantly significant of the substantial nature of Rock Hill's prosperity.

## FIRST NATIONAL BANK.

The First National Bank was organized January 15, 1887, with a capital of $50,000. The officers first elected were: W. L. Roddey, President; John R. London, Vice-President; W. J. Roddey, Cashier; J. H. Miller, Teller.

The present capital is $75,000, with a surplus and profits of $29,000 and deposits amounting to $121,000.

The following gentlemen compose the present Board of Directors: W. L. Roddey, John R. London, J. E. Roddey, A. F. Ruff, W. A. Watson, W. J. Roddey and J. H. Miller.

Present Officers: W. L. Roddey, President; W. J. Roddey, Vice-President; J. H. Miller, Cashier; R. Lee Kerr, Teller.

## THE SAVINGS BANK.

This bank was organized in 1886, with a capital of $22,000. It now has a capital of $50,000, with surplus and profits of $28,250, and deposits of $111,000.

The Board of Directors of the Savings Bank are: D. Hutchison, Jno. R. London, T. L. Johnson, W. J. Rawlinson, W. C. Hutchison, R. T. Fewell and Dr. T. A. Crawford.

Officers: D. Hutchison, President; Jno. R. London, Vice-President; J. M. Cherry, Cashier.

The foregoing figures show that both of these banks are in a flourishing condition. The apartments of the First National, on the first floor of the Roddey building, are tastily finished and decorated, and provided with costly and elegant office fixtures and furniture. The Savings Bank building, on Main Street, has an iron and plate glass front, and is one of the prettiest business houses in the city. Its interior design, finish and furnishings are in keeping with the outside appearance.

## ROCK HILL REAL ESTATE AND LOAN COMPANY.

This institution was organized in 1890. Its authorized capital is $100,000. Of this, $76,200 was subscribed. The par value of the shares is $100 each, made payable in monthly instalments of one dollar per share. The history of this company, which is but a repetition of the history of the Savings Bank, shows how salaried men, and others of small income, with nothing to invest, may become capitalists. It is a short story, and means simply the putting aside of part of one's wages or earnings, whatever can be conveniently spared, monthly, and permitting it to accumulate and become, with other funds built up in the same way, organized and efficient capital. He is thus, scarcely knowing how or why, a stockholder in a financial institution, receiving dividends and at the same time building up his city.

The amount paid in by the subscribers to this company, together with the earnings of the company, is now sufficient to make the stock worth $100 per share. The fully paid capital is therefore $76,200.

After thus seeing that this company has matured its stock in seventy-nine months, nothing need be said about the success of the plan.

The Board of Directors of this company is composed of the following gentlemen : D. Hutchison, J. R. London, A. Friedheim, R. T. Fewell, T. L. Johnson, W. J. Rawlinson, J. M. Cherry, M. H. Sandifer and J. B. Johnson.

The Officers are: D. Hutchison, President; W. J. Rawlinson, Vice-President, and J. M. Cherry, Secretary and Treasurer.

RAIL ROAD AVENUE.
LOOKING EAST.

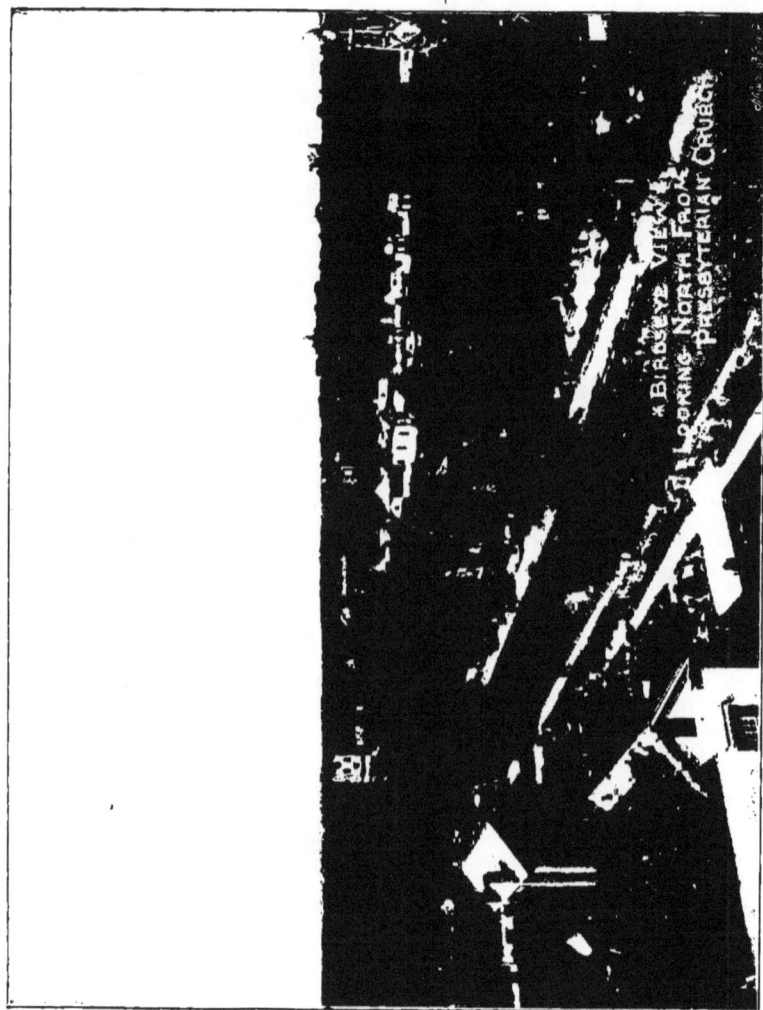

*BIRDSEYE VIEW. LOOKING NORTH FROM PRESBYTERIAN CHURCH*

### SOUTHERN LOAN AND INVESTMENT COMPANY.

This company was organized in 1888, and has a paid up capital of $75,000. Its business is buying, selling and improving real estate.

The Officers of this company are: W. L. Roddey, President; W. J. Roddey, Manager.

This organization is prospering, and doing its part in building up city and country.

### MUTUAL HOME BUILDING AND LOAN ASSOCIATION.

This is what its name implies, a building and loan association, and is run entirely by home capital and home men. Its capital stock is $42,000, which is paid in instalments and loaned out to the members on first mortgage real estate securities. It is doing a good business, and has several comfortable and attractive little homes to its credit in the city.

It was organized in May, 1892, with the following Officers : John R. London, President ; J. B. Johnson, Vice-President ; R. Lee Kerr, Secretary and Treasurer.

● ●

# Insurance.

Most of the standard life insurance companies are represented by live agents in Rock Hill. Life insurance has gained a prominence at this point, and this field has engaged some of the best talent of the city.

### THE EQUITABLE IN THE CAROLINAS.

The General Agency of the Equitable for the Carolinas is located at Rock Hill, and Mr. W. J. Roddey, a young man of large experience and fine executive ability, is at the head. Mr. Roddey's quick rise from the ranks to the head of his calling shows his worth as an insurance man. In 1888, he was the local agent for the Equitable; in January, 1889, he accepted the State Agency in connection with A. J. Clark, of Lancaster, S. C. ; in July, 1889, he bought Clark out and

13

became the General Agent for the State; in January, 1890, the State of North Carolina was added to his territory, making him General Agent for the Carolinas, under Geo. T. G. White, Southern Manager; in 1891, the office of General Southern Manager was abolished and Mr. Roddey was appointed by the home office for the Carolinas.

When Mr. Roddey went into the insurance business a new impetus was given to it in this section. He has always pushed his business, and is now travelling a large number of agents in his territory. He has large and commodious offices in the Roddey building, which are elegantly furnished, and he employs a large number of clerks, stenographers and assistants.

Mr. Roddey is a progresive citizen and has been prominently identified with Rock Hill's history in the last decade.

### NEW YORK LIFE.

This strong company is ably represented by Mr. David Hutchison, and does a good business. Mr. Hutchison employs several sub-agents in the life insurance business. He can tell you all about life insurance and can furnish a policy to suit the most fastidious.

Mr. Hutchison and Mr. W. J. Roddey each represent strong and popular fire insurance companies, and do an extensive fire insurance business. There are other fire insurance agents who do business in the city.

● ●

## Educational.

### THE ROCK HILL GRADED SCHOOL.

The first step in the direction of public education taken by the municipal authorities of Rock Hill was the establishment of the Rock Hill Graded School. The citizens, several years ago, felt that it was not only important, but actually necessary that better educational advantages should be provided for their children, and this feeling soon crystallized in the shape of a large two-story, brick, school building, with handsome superintendent's residence appurtenant. The school building is conveniently located on a pretty site in the southeastern portion of the city, and presents a neat and attractive appearance. It is commodious, well arranged and well ventilated, its construction being on late improved plans; and it is suitably equipped with modern school furniture and proper teaching appliances. It contains seven large class rooms, with a large auditorium in the second story, capable of seating several hundred people. The superintendent's residence is an eight room, frame building, conveniently located on the school grounds.

The first bonded indebtedness of the town was incurred for the purpose of this school, it being built with the proceeds of seven thousand dollars of town bonds, issued in 1888, supplemented by a fund of fifteen hundred dollars, which was a private donation.

This school opened September 3, 1888, with one hundred and twenty-five pupils. It now has a yearly enrolment of more than four hundred. It teaches primary and high school branches, and confers certificates. It is at present under the efficient superintendence of Professor J. W. Thomson, an experienced educator, who is assisted by an able complement of teachers for the different grades.

The Board of Trustees is composed of the following gentlemen : Iredell Jones, Chairman ; A. E. Smith, Secretary and Treasurer; Capt. W. L. Roddey, W. B. Wilson, W. S. Creighton, J. M. Cherry and Col. J. J. Waters.

There are several private schools where the primary branches are taught, and there is a separate graded school for colored children. It is proposed also to conduct another graded school in connection with the Winthrop Normal and Industrial College.

## HIGH SCHOOL.

The Rock Hill High School embraces the idea of a connecting link between the graded school and the college or university. It commences where the graded school ends, and prepares students for entering the higher college or university classes. It also equips them for the ordinary pursuits of life. The High School building is an imposing brick structure situated on Oakland Heights, commanding a splendid view of the city and of the community around. It was built at a cost of $22,000. It is equipped with a large two-story brick dormitory, and suitable educational appliances.

This school was built by the Presbyterians of Rock Hill, assisted by Bethel Presbytery. While it is thus under the special care of the Presbyterian Denomination, it is not sectarian in character, and it is patronized by students of other religious denominations.

This school opened with bright prospects in 1892, under the Principalship of Prof. A. R. Banks, an educator of large experience. It will doubtless become an important factor in the educational advancement of the city.

## THE WINTHROP NORMAL AND INDUSTRIAL COLLEGE.

It will not do to say that up to this time South Carolinians have neglected the higher education of women. There have for many years been a number of well equipped private colleges and higher institutions of learning where their daughters could be educated; but it is true, nevertheless, that the State, in its corporate capacity, has, until recently, completely ignored this matter.

Nothing was heard of a separate State institution for girls until Hon. W. S. Hall, a member of the State Legislature from Chester County, introduced a bill, in 1883, to provide for State aid in the education of white women. The matter was indefinitely postponed by the Legislature.

Again, in 1885, a concurrent resolution was adopted, " instructing the committee on education of the two houses to prepare a plan whereby suitable provision shall be made for the education of the white female children of the State." This resolution resulted in nothing except to expand the growing sentiment for a college for girls.

In 1886, Prof. D. B. Johnson, Superintendent of the Columbia Graded Schools, being imbued with the idea of a training school for

GRADED SCHOOL.

HIGH SCHOOL.

teachers in these schools, went North and secured from the Peabody Fund an appropriation of about $2,000 for this normal school. In this, he had the hearty coöperation of Hon. Robert C. Winthrop, Chairman of the Trustees of the Peabody Fund, and of Dr. J. L. M. Curry, the General Agent of this fund.

On November 15, 1886, the Training School for young white women of South Carolina was organized at Columbia, and it was named in honor of the illustrious President of the Board of the Peabody Educational Fund, who was always a friend to the cause of education in the South.

The first Board of Trustees of this school consisted of F. W. McMaster, Chairman ; R. L. Bryan, Wm. H. Lyles, W. C. Swaffield, Jno. P. Thomas, Jr., Edward S. Joynes, W. J. Duffie and D. B. Johnson.

The first Faculty was : D. B. Johnson, President ; Miss M. H. Leonard, Principal; Miss A. E. Bonham, Practice Teacher; Mrs. T. C. Robertson, Teacher of Drawing.

Seventeen young ladies entered this school at the opening, and this number grew to twenty-one, fourteen of whom finished the course and received diplomas the first year.

The Winthrop Training School was chartered by the Legislature in December, 1887 ; its sole declared purpose being the training of teachers; and about $5,100 was appropriated for its use by the State. This, with the $2,000 derived from the Peabody Fund, represented the inadequate sum with which this institution began its work.

In July, 1890, Dr. Edward S. Joynes, of the South Carolina College, in a speech at Florence, S. C., spoke of the importance of a college for women, combining industrial and normal features, and said that honor awaited the Governor who first recommended it, and the Legislature by which it was created.

Hon. John Peter Richardson, while Governor, favored it in his messages to the Legislature; and, when retiring from office in 1890, spoke of it as a necessity, and of the neglect of proper female education as a reproach to the State.

Governor B. R. Tillman, in his inaugural address, delivered December 4, 1890, made a strong plea for industrial education for the girls of the State, and offered some very practical suggestions looking to definite action. The result was that, through the aid of the Legislature, a Commission composed of Prof. D. B. Johnson, of Columbia, Miss Hannah Hemphill, of Abbeville, and Miss May L. Yeargin, of Laurens, was appointed to visit the leading institutions of the North, to ascertain if normal and industrial education could be profitably carried on together. This Commission reported favorably, and the Act of the Legislature of December, 1891, followed, creating "The Winthrop Normal and Industrial College of South Carolina." Under this Act the Winthrop Training School was accepted by the State and merged into the College.

The Act provides for the management of the College by a Board of Trustees composed of the Governor, State Superintendent of Education, the Chairman of the Committee on Education of the Senate and House, and nine other members, seven to be elected by the Legislature, and two more residing where the College is located, to be elected by the Trustees.

Pursuant to the terms of the Act, the Trustees advertised for bids, to be made by counties and municipalities in the State and paid in money or bonds, and were required to locate the College at the place offering the greatest advantages.

Rock Hill held an election on March 27, 1893; voted a subscription of $60,000 in bonds, guaranteed at par; donated a splendid site of thirty and one-fourth acres of the best property in the corporate limits; contributed $700 in cash, and 375,000 brick, delivered, and secured the prize.

No stronger testimonial of the enterprise and pluck of Rock Hill can be given than to state the fact that she secured this important institution in the face of the most formidable opposition, wrenching it from the grasp of all her competitors among the most enterprising, populous and wealthy cities of the State.

The College building, just completed, is the finest of its kind in the South, and would be a credit to any city. It is situated in Oakland, one of Rock Hill's most delightful suburbs, on an eminence overlooking the city; and in the beauty of its architectural design, as well as in the convenience of its arrangement in matters of detail, cannot be excelled. It fronts on Oakland Avenue, an elegant driveway, and on either wing the plan is for a large brick dormitory, though only one of these has been completed. The dormitory that has been finished is fitted up with all modern conveniences, and the comfort of the young ladies has received most careful consideration in its arrangements and appliances. The College has a complete system of water works of its own. Macadamized driveways extend all around the College grounds. The cost of the buildings and equipments will, completed, approximate a quarter of a million dollars.

As the name of the College indicates, it is an institution where South Carolina girls may be educated, while trained at the same time in the industrial arts, and where they may be fitted for the noble profession of teaching. In the language of its efficient President, D. B. Johnson, "The institution will aim to join the 'cultured mind' with the 'skilful hand,' and have both dominated by the 'good heart.'"

A system of scholarships has been provided for the College, and it will be liberally supported by the State. The expenses of board, tuition and incidentals will be small; and no tuition will be required from pupils who are unable to pay.

When the second dormitory shall have been finished, between five and six hundred young ladies can be accommodated.

The College opened October 15, of the present year, and more than three hundred applications for admission have been made.

This article will show that President D. B. Johnson has always been identified with the history of the College. He is a scholarly and polished gentleman, with the cause of higher female education thoroughly at heart, and the Board has acted wisely in placing him at the head of the faculty. The entire faculty is an able one, made up of the best talent in the country.

The following gentlemen constitute the present Board of Trustees: John Gary Evans, Governor; W. D. Mayfield, Superintendent of Education ; W. A. Brown, Chairman of Senate Committee on Education ; J. E. Ellerbee, Chairman of House Committee on Education; J. E. Brazeale, E. S. Joynes, W. N. Elder, D. W. McLaurin, A. C. Fuller, A. H. Patterson, H. B. Buist, B. R. Tillman, W. J. Roddey and T. A. Crawford.

Such is a brief outline sketch of this noble institution, which is the pride of the State. Further comment is unnecessary. It marks a new era for South Carolina womanhood. The State has gloriously redeemed herself, and Rock Hill is delighted with the honor of having contributed to the result.

● ●

## Moral and Religious.

Rock Hill is a well-behaved place. The people are sober and peaceable, and society is high-toned and moral. The rum traffic was forever blotted from Rock Hill's history in the year 1881, when by a special act of the Legislature, the sale of intoxicating liquors was prohibited. The young men of the city are thus removed from temptation, and are usually employed in some honorable business. They have higher ideals of living than such as the cup of pleasure affords, and are mostly young men of affairs.

Rock Hill people go to church; and there are, among the white people, churches for four denominations: Presbyterian, Methodist, Baptist and Episcopalian. Two factory chapels have been erected under the auspices of the Presbyterian Church, known respectively as "White Memorial" and "Jennings" Chapels. There are about an equal number of churches for colored people.

Members of the Associate Reformed Presbyterian Church worship in one of the city halls. This denomination will erect an attractive house of worship in the city at an early day.

The Presbyterians, only a few months ago, finished a handsome new church on Main Street. It is beautiful in design, convenient and comfortable, and is an ornament to the city. It was built at a cost of $12,000. The Presbyterian denomination is the strongest in the city, having a membership of over four hundred and eighty.

The Baptists have also recently built a pretty and inviting little church, which is pleasantly situated on Hampton Street.

The Methodist congregation will enlarge and improve its present house of worship.

A spirit of harmony prevails in all the churches, and they are in a prosperous condition, keeping pace with the city's general advancement.

• •

# Ibealtb.

Rock Hill is situated near the foot of the Blue Ridge Mountains on the highest elevation between Columbia and Charlotte, being 668 feet above tide water. The water is pure free-stone, and there are no malarial troubles. The city is kept scrupulously clean, and the best sanitary regulations are rigidly enforced.

Hence the health of the city has always been good, and no epidemics or diseases of an endemic character have ever been known.

### MINERAL SPRINGS.

There are several mineral springs in the vicinity of Rock Hill, but the most noted is the one known as "Steele's Spring," owned by John G. Steele, of Rock Hill, and situated a short distance beyond the corporate limits. It has been analyzed, and contains valuable medicinal ingredients, among which are magnesium, sodium, sulphates, silica, alumina, calcium and potassium.

Mr. Steele has the spring neatly fitted up, and daily supplies a large number of the citizens with water. This water is most beneficial in cases of dyspepsia and kidney diseases, and its curative qualities have made for it a reputation abroad, orders for shipments being often received by the owner.

# The People.

The people of Rock Hill are unique, and the only way to know them thoroughly is to come and mingle with them. Their predominant characteristic is, perhaps, the belief that nothing is too good for them, and nothing unattainable. They are not disciples of the school whose maxim is, "Blessed are those who expect nothing." Theirs is, "Blessed are those who expect the best of all that is good," and the truth of this dogma of theirs is in the fact that they have had many good things and are sure of "more." What they do get is obtained fairly, and as a consequence of labor and a laudable ambition. They are not wanting in any of the valuable traits which are peculiar to a refined and cultured people.

Here is what has been said of the people by an outsider: "Although Rock Hill owes its progress so far entirely to Southern enterprise and energy, its people are not at all narrow-minded or illiberal. Desirable citizens, from whatever section, will here find a most cordial welcome. They are offered the highest and purest moral, social, educational and religious, as well as first-class business advantages. The courteous hospitality with which the Rock Hill people have ever treated her guests has become proverbial, and not a single blot is on her fair name."

## RESIDENCES AND BUSINESS HOUSES.

The people of Rock Hill do not all live in gilded palaces, or even in mansions. There are nevertheless many costly and handsome residences, and the people generally are comfortably and attractively housed. More attention is being paid to fine residences than ever before, and many splendid homes are now building in the new site of Oakland, spoken of elsewhere.

The business houses are all of brick, large, comely and convenient; and some of the store-rooms of Rock Hill are as large and present as attractive an interior as those of any city in the State.

# Lodges.

There are lodges of different orders in Rock Hill as follows: Masonic, Knights of Honor, Legion of Honor, Knights of Pythias, Order of the Golden Chain, and Woodmen of the World. All of these lodges have good memberships.

• •

# Catawba Club.

This is the leading social organization of the city. It is regularly chartered, has apartments elegantly fitted up and furnished, with reading and sitting rooms and a billiard and pool room. It is supplied with periodicals and the leading daily papers. It is governed by a rigid code of laws, and the strictest decorum is required on its premises.

There are Chautauquan and other literary societies in the city.

• •

# Hotels.

Very often an object is good, bad or indifferent, according to the point of view from which it is considered ; and doubtless that large class of travelling men who have to do with hotels will be disposed to base their estimate of a place, to some extent, upon its hotel accommodations. And doubtless, too, a hotel is often a correct index to the character of a town or city. There is an inspiration of progressiveness about a live town, and a hotel must catch it or be lost in the race of life. Rock Hill has never suffered because of her hotel accommodations.

Located in a section where the most delicious beef, pork and mutton can be had for "a song," and where milk and butter and eggs and fat chickens are cheap and plentiful, and where every wagon from the country is a portable market in itself for supplying the wants of the city, no difficulty is had in procuring and preparing edible and palatable dishes for the table. Hence Rock Hill has always had the reputation of feeding guests.

23

## THE CAROLINA.

While the cuisine of this hotel is always of a high standard, its management realizes that "man does not live by bread alone," and that there are many other matters necessary to the make-up of a first-class hotel. Mr. A. H. Greene, of the Carolina, is a master of the art, and knows exactly what is required in the business. The hotel building is of brick, three stories high, situated on Main Street within a stone's throw of the passenger depot of the Southern Railway. It is an imposing structure, and contains forty elegantly and comfortably furnished rooms. It is equipped with electric call bells, speaking tubes, telephone, baths, etc. Competent servants administer to the comfort of the guests, and experienced cooks are in charge of the culinary department.

The hunting privileges of the Carolina are worthy of more than a passing notice. This section offers peculiar and special advantages for sportsmen, and these advantages are improved by many Northern gentlemen, who visit Rock Hill during the winter months. The Carolina Hotel posesses shooting privileges for its guests over 12,000 acres of land; and for persons fond of quail and snipe shooting, a veritable paradise is here found. It is not unusual for two good shots to bag from 60 to 75 quail in a day. Woodcock is also found here; and thousands of geese and ducks have their haunts, in winter, along the Catawba River, within a convenient distance of the city.

The first floor of the hotel building is occupied by the hotel office, the First National Bank, and the large and pretty store of the Roddey Mercantile Company. This building was erected by Captain W. L. Roddey, in 1888, at a cost of $18,000. It is known as the "Roddey Building."

## THE CENTRAL.

This is a two-story hotel conveniently located on Main Street, and is conducted by Mrs. M. Sadler. This hotel is well kept, but does not cater for the transient trade, being principally devoted to regular boarders.

TOBACCO FIELD

Besides these, there are a number of private boarding houses in the city where good board can be had at low rates, and Rock Hill can always take care of her guests. When necessary for their accommodation, the hospitable homes of the citizens are thrown open to strangers and a welcome given.

● ●

## Market.

Rock Hill has always held high rank as a cotton market, and yields not to Charlotte, Augusta, or any other point on the Charlotte, Columbia and Augusta Railroad, in the price paid. On account of her cotton factories consuming a large proportion of the cotton raised in this section, the price is often greater than can be realized on shipments, giving an advantage both to the city and the cotton growers around.

A lively market is also afforded for the sale of all kinds of produce; and truck farming in this section, still in its incipiency, presents an inviting field to such as have tastes leading them in that direction.

● ●

## Manufacturing.

### COTTON.

"Cotton mills among the cotton fields" used to be a theory, but is now become a condition. As to the manufacture of the coarser grades of cotton fabrics, New England's occupation is gone, and the business now belongs to "Dixie-land." More capital and skilled labor are all that are needed to place the South on the topmost round of cotton manufacturing of every grade and quality.

Rock Hill, a number of years ago, believed that the conditions for cotton spinning and weaving in the Piedmont Belt were favorable; thought that the business could be done by steam power, made the experiment and proved the wisdom of her speculations.

This was among the first towns in the State to build a cotton mill, and the success of Rock Hill's first mill—the Rock Hill Cotton Factory—was such that others followed and are still following in rapid succession.

All of Rock Hill's factories have made money; two of the three in operation have paid dividends, and the third could have done so had not its earnings been applied to improving its machinery and enlarging the plant. Besides these benefits to the stockholders, the indirect advantages accruing to the city in the large amount of money thrown into the channels of trade, and to planters of the country around in having a better market for their cotton and other products, are not to be passed unnoticed.

Rock Hill has profited in the various ways suggested, and she is still pushing forward on the lines begun, feeling assured that her conquests are not yet complete in this field.

## THE ROCK HILL COTTON FACTORY.

This mill was incorporated in the year 1880, and began operations the year following. The capital stock is $100,000, divided into shares of the par value of $100. The factory building is a large and attractive two-story brick structure, conveniently located near the intersection of the Southern and Ohio River and Charleston Railroads, with each of which roads it has rail connections for the purposes of receiving and delivering freight. It was devoted exclusively to spinning up to 1894, when the Directors decided to put in looms, and it now has 8,000 spindles and 200 looms. The value of this plant at present is $175,000. It consumes about 2,500 bales of cotton per annum, and its products are yarns and white goods—shirtings, sheetings and drills. Its products find a ready market at the North. It employs 175 hands, and its weekly pay-roll is about $625.

This mill is running regularly, and it pays its stockholders an annual dividend of seven per cent.

Its Board of Directors are: A. E. Hutchison, A. H. White, W. L. Roddey, J. R. London, W. B. Fewell, F. J. Pelzer, of Charleston, and Jno. Gill, of Baltimore.

Officers: A. E. Hutchison, President; D. Hutchison, Secretary.

## STANDARD COTTON MILL.

This factory furnishes an object lesson on what can be done in factory building by the instalment plan. The authorized capital is $150,000; made payable by the stockholders in instalments of fifty cents per week on each share. The mill was organized in March, 1888, and $71,000 of the capital stock was immediately subscribed. Funds were secured by the directors, and the building of the mill was commenced shortly after the organization. The plant was ready and operations were commenced February 29, 1889, with 200 looms, weaving alone being the business of this factory. In 1891, the number of looms was increased to 300; and this number was again increased, in 1892 and 1893, to 486. The present value of the plant is $150,000. The products of this mill are fine gingham goods, shirtings, towels, etc., and the value of the yearly output is $300,000. It employs 280 hands, and has a weekly pay-roll of $1,100.

The subscribed capital was fully paid several years ago; additional stock has since been subscribed and paid, and the value of the plant largely increased, as appears above. It is now paying to its stockholders a ten per cent. annual dividend. This factory occupies a large two-story brick building in the eastern suburbs of the city, near the Ohio River and Charleston Railroad, with which it has a rail connection.

The Board of Directors are : W. L. Roddey, A. Friedheim, J. R. London, R. T. Fewell, J. B. Johnson, W. J. Roddey, W. J. Rawlinson, T. A. Crawford, A. E. Smith.

Officers : Jno. R. London, President and Treasurer ; P. C. Poag, Secretary.

Only one change has been made among the officers of this mill since its organization, and that has been on account of death.

## GLOBE MILL.

The Globe is a spinning and weaving mill, and has 7,380 spindles and 320 looms. It occupies a one-story brick building, 375 feet long and 120 feet wide, situated on the Southern Railway, in the southeastern portion of the city.

This mill was chartered in 1889, its authorized capital being $100,-000. Of this amount, $95,000 was immediately subscribed and paid, and the factory commenced operations in 1890. The plant is now valued at $110,000. Its products are yarns and fine dress ginghams. It consumes 1,800 bales of cotton per annum, 325 operatives are employed, and the weekly pay-roll amounts to $1,200.

This factory has been profitably operated, but its earnings have been applied to improvements and new machinery, and not to paying dividends. The products of both the Globe and Standard Mills find a ready sale in the Northern markets.

The Directors of the Globe are: W. L. Roddey, A. Friedheim, J. R. London, A. E. Smith, A. F. Ruff, R. T. Fewell and J. N. Trainer.

Officers: John R. London, President and Treasurer ; P. C. Poag, Secretary.

## THE ARCADE MILL.

Here again is an object lesson, showing what one live, energetic, ambitious citizen can accomplish in a community ; for it cannot be gainsaid that Mr. R. T. Fewell is the leading spirit in this enterprise, and that its assured success is due largely to his indomitable pluck and perseverance. In fact, it is known as the " Fewell Mill," and the honor is well merited.

The authorized capital of this mill is $200,000, and $100,000 has already been subscribed and paid. The building of the mill and houses for the hands has already commenced, and it is estimated that the plant will be finished and ready for operations by the first of February, 1896. The factory building will be of brick, two stories, and will be 226 feet long and 79 feet wide. The mill will begin work with 6,500 spindles and 180 looms. It is estimated that it will consume between 1,800 and 2,000 bales of cotton per annum, employ about 200 hands, and have a weekly pay-roll of between $800 and $1,000. This mill will manufacture gray goods of the kind used for converters.

BAPTIST
CHURCH

These goods will be shipped to the Northern markets, where there is always a demand for them.

The Board of Directors are: R. T. Fewell, J. M. Cherry, T. L. Johnson, W. J. Roddey, W. J. Rawlinson, T. A. Crawford, Julius Friedheim. Mr. R. T. Fewell is President and Treasurer.

## THE MANCHESTER MILL.

Here is another achievement of a plucky man with brains in his head. It is Mr. J. R. Barron's handsome tribute to a live city. That Mr. Fewell and Mr. Barron, each of whom are still on the sunny side of life's meridian, should have had the hardihood to set out to build two cotton factories, in the same municipality, in sight of each other, and this on the heels of a panic that has seriously damaged the cotton milling interests all over the country, is a straw to show how the wind blows. It shows that there is life in this old land yet, that there is faith in Rock Hill, and that cotton manufacturing properly belongs to the land "where the cotton whitens beneath the stars."

The Manchester will be a three-story building, and will present a handsome appearance when completed. Work has already been begun, and the plant will be ready for operations in the Spring of 1896.

The capital invested is $125,000, and it will begin with 7,000 spindles and 200 looms. It will consume between 1,800 and 2,000 bales of cotton yearly, will employ about 200 hands, and the weekly pay-roll will be between $750 and $1,000. The products will be yarns and white goods.

The Board of Directors are: J. R. Barron, W. L. Roddey, J. Freidheim, J. B. Johnson, W. J. Roddey, R. L. Campbell, of Clover, S. C., E. Milheiser, of Richmond, Va., and Robert H. Wylie, of New York.

Mr. J. R. Barron is President and Treasurer.

## THE ROCK HILL BUGGY COMPANY.

This corporation was chartered in 1886, and has a capital stock of $75,000. It does a yearly business of from sixty to seventy-five thousand dollars; employs 65 men; travels two men on the road all the time, and sells vehicles all through the South and West. It employs the latest improved modern machinery. Its immense plant covers four acres. This is one of the gigantic institutions of Rock Hill, and its vehicles have made for it an enviable reputation wherever they have been introduced.

The Directors are: A. R. Smith, J. M. Cherry, D. Hutchison, A. D. Holler, Sam Friedheim, W. J. Roddey, T. A. Crawford, Frel Mobley and Jno. G. Anderson.

Officers: A. R. Smith, President ; D. Hutchison, Vice-President ; J. M. Cherry, Treasurer; John G. Anderson, Manager.

## DOOR, SASH AND BLIND.

The L. L. Clyburn Door, Sash and Blind Factory is not to be overlooked. The name of this factory sufficiently indicates its object. Captain L. L. Clyburn is sole proprietor, and the capital invested is $20,000. About 25 hands are employed, and the weekly pay-roll is something like a hundred dollars. This factory contracts also to build houses.

## PIEDMONT TOBACCO WORKS.

This factory was chartered the present year, and is in operation at present with a full force of hands. It is authorized under its charter to engage in the manufacture of tobacco in every conceivable form. Its authorized capital is $40,000, the greater part of which has been subscribed and paid. This factory is at present engaged exclusively in the manufacture of plug and twist tobacco, and it turns out several grades, its products comparing favorably with those of experienced manufacturers of the tobacco states. It will consume 230,000 pounds of crude tobacco yearly, and the proceeds from its annual products will not fall short of $30,000. It employs 100 hands, and has a weekly pay-roll of $300. It employs both skilled and unskilled labor, hence there is much difference in the wages paid. Expert rollers are paid from $10 to $15 per week.

This factory is located in Rock Hill because of the recent extensive operations in tobacco culture in this section; of which something will be hereafter stated. It has bright promises of success. Mr. Philip Taylor, an experienced tobacconist, formerly of North Carolina, is in charge as President.

The Board of Directors are: Philip Taylor, Dr. T. A. Crawford, John R. London, W. J. Roddey, J. B. Johnson, D. Hutchison and Frel Mobley.

## MISCELLANEOUS MANUFACTURING.

In addition to the manufacturing industries thus briefly described, there are others worthy of mention. There are machine shops which are doing a prosperous business, in connection with which is an iron foundry.

The Egypt Canning Company cans vegetables and fruits, and its products are of a high grade and find ready sale in the home market as well as abroad.

There are tile and brick factories, which make most of the brick used in Rock Hill and are kept busily employed.

There are flouring mills which produce a fine quality of flour from wheat raised in this section, the products being sold in competition with those of Western mills.

Superior saddles and harness are manufactured, and orders for these articles from different parts of the State are filled.

A movement is on foot for the establishment of a cotton seed oil mill, which is a possibility of the near future. Rock Hill has already had an oil mill, but the plant was recently destroyed by fire. Its success when in operation was sufficient to induce the building of another, which will soon be accomplished.

## LANDS-FORD ELECTRIC POWER PLANT.

One of the mammoth enterprises which promises much for Rock Hill is the certain early development of the water-power at the Lands-Ford Falls of the Catawba River, than which there is probably no greater in the Union. These falls cover a wide space of ground, and onsequently the rise in freshets is never great. The drainage area above Lands-Ford is about 3,425 square miles, hence these ample water powers are continuous.

In 1820, the State of South Carolina built a canal nearly two miles long, covering the distance around these falls, for boating purposes. This canal was built at a large expense, and still shows evidences of superior masonry in its construction. It is still standing, and with a little repairing, can be made to render good service in carrying water for turning mills. It was built of granite obtained from quarries near by, and plenty of granite is still there to serve its part in factory building. At the head of this canal a curved dam of loose rock, 4½ feet high, now extends across to an island, a distance of about 1,500 feet. This dam raises the water only about 2½ feet. The fall in this canal, exclusive of the guard-lock, is about 35 feet; with a tight dam six or eight feet high at the head of the canal, a fall of 40 feet can be obtained.

A responsible engineer, after a thorough examination, estimates that 15,000 horse-power can be developed at this place at a comparatively small cost. In addition to this, there are many natural advantges to be considered, such as freedom from ice stoppage in winter; splendid factory sites, with rock foundations for buildings and machinery; the best building materials immediately at hand; no reservoir to watch, etc.

This water-power is situated at a distance of fifteen miles from Rock Hill, southeast, and is controlled by Rock Hill capitalists. A company has been organized and operations will be commenced at an early day, and it is expected that the plant will be completed and ready for business in the Spring of 1896. The plan of its promoters is to establish a large electric power plant at Lands-Ford and transmit electricity to Rock Hill for the supply of the various factories and machinery here located. It is estimated that 2,500 horse-power can be delivered at Rock Hill from a plant built at a cost of $250,000, and the company has already a guaranty of having to supply 2,000 horse-power to Rock Hill manufacturers at the price of $30,000 per annum.

EPISTORAL CHURCH

Rock Hill
Cotton Factory

In addition to the enterprise already outlined, this company will build cotton and other factories on the river, and will sell factory sites to persons or companies who wish to avail themselves of the many fine advantages offered.

A writer, in speaking of this subject, shows the superior advantages of Lands-Ford by comparison with other places, and particularly with Augusta, Ga. He says:

"The canal at Augusta is seven miles long, and has cost $822,000. The price paid for the use of the power, undeveloped, is $5.50 per annum, for each horse power. There are about 160,000 spindles and about 4,000 looms in operation up to this date in that enterprising and attractive city. This grand canal and power is the source of Augusta's growth and industrial prosperity; from the point of view of an investment, it is proper to state that the canal's annual rentals show an income of 10 per cent. on its total cost.

"A manufacturing and power company will be able to locate, along one and one-fourth miles of this proposed canal at Lands-Ford, six separate mills and mill villages, with a total of 200,000 spindles and 5,000 looms, and furnish water to turn their wheels, on an outlay of about $80,000, which is less than one-tenth the outlay at Augusta, and can furnish additional power for electrical purposes."

● ●

## Tobacco Culture.

In the year 1893, tobacco growing was attempted on a small scale in this section as an experiment. Several farmers of the community joined together, each planting small areas, and the services of T. S. Groome, an experienced tobacco raiser of North Carolina, were secured. The test was sufficient to insure more extensive planting the second year, and Mr. Frel Mobley, a live and energetic young Rock Hillian, who knows a good thing when he sees it, took Mr. Groome into co-partnership and planted a large area in tobacco. These young men were successful, and realized a neat profit from their crop of 1894. There was no longer a doubt as to the advantages of tobacco raising in this section; and Messrs. Mobley and Groome this year manage and control two hundred acres of land planted in tobacco, distributed between Catawba and Bethsda Townships. Their crop is a good average one, and will yield about 700 pounds per acre, of fine texture and good color. They have employed four expert curers for the present crop, and have arranged for fifteen experienced graders to grade the crop before it is placed on the market. They will have between thirty-five and forty thousand pounds ready for market by the first day of November, and are assured of a very handsome profit from the present crop. Messrs. Mobley and Groome are well provided with barns, flues, warehouses, stripping rooms and cellars.

Besides the acreage cultivated by these gentlemen, there are about one hundred acres cultivated by others, making about three hundred acres employed in tobacco culture. The success of this experiment has been so great, and the proceeds to be realized from the present crop will be so large, that the tobacco acreage of 1896 will probably be double that of this year.

The loamy, sandy soil of this section is specially adapted to the production of wrappers, and the leaves are lemon and bright yellow in color. Experts who have examined the tobacco, say that the quality cannot be excelled anywhere. The best grade sells for $75.00 per hundred pounds, and the average price realized from a crop is from 10 to 12½ cents per pound.

A comparison of the foregoing figures with those presented in cotton raising makes the importance of this industry apparent. Experienced tobacco planters, who have also engaged in raising cotton, say that the cost per acre of raising a tobacco crop is only four dollars more than the cost per acre of raising a cotton crop. The profits from a tobacco farm, where properly managed, are easily double and sometimes triple what the profits of the same farm would be in cotton. So that the kingship of cotton is in peril; and this other product, which may now be regarded as staple in this section, is bidding for the supremacy with every indication in its favor.

# Labor and Wages.

Some idea of the amount of wages paid to the laborer will doubtless be gathered from the preceding pages. Unskilled labor is practically represented by colored people, and skilled labor by white. Unskilled labor receives from 75 cents to $1.00 per day, while skilled labor is paid from $1.50 to $4.00 per day. Laborers all find plenty of work, and none are idle from necessity.

• •

# Real Estate.

## ROCK HILL LAND AND TOWN SITE COMPANY.

The increasing demand for dwelling houses and building sites in Rock Hill a few years ago impressed some of her enterprising citizens with the imperative necessity of providing for these exigencies of a growing municipality. Hence the Rock Hill Land and Town Site Company was organized in 1891, with the following Directors : W. B. Wilson, President; R. T. Fewell, Vice-President; W. L. Roddey, Treasurer; J. M. Cherry, Secretary; Jno. J. Hemphill.

This company purchased a large body of land adjacent to that part of the city which was already built up and improved, most of which was within, but some without the corporate limits. This property is situated north of the business portion of the city, on a high elevation, and could not have been better selected for the purpose intended. The Town Site Company has a capital of $100,000, and they have spared no expense necessary to the improvement of this property. Broad streets and drive-ways have been graded through the property and named ; lots have been surveyed and numbered ; and descriptive maps have been published, showing outlines, streets, measurements, lots, sites, etc. A public park, intersected with drive-ways and containing a pleasure pavilion, is one of the attractions, and it all goes to make up the pleasing little village of Oakland.

## OAKLAND.

"Going out to Oakland" is a popular expression in Rock Hill, and the city is becoming so fond of drifting in that direction that the City Street Railway, which extends through and connects Oakland with the business section, is destined before long to reap a rich harvest. In fact, the Street Railway is a product of Oakland and has had the same promoters. The Industrial College and the High School are situated in Oakland, in sight of each other, and large and beautiful residences are springing up all over this lovely suburban village.

Oakland is the work of the Town Site Company, and the success of this venture proves the wisdom of its promoters.

This company held a public auction of city lots on the 3d and 4th days of July, 1891, when a number of lots were sold. It has still many valuable building lots, which are offered at reasonable rates. This property is certain to enhance in value; and there can be no doubt about the growth of Oakland as a part of Rock Hill, and on account of the special educational advantages afforded.

## IREDELL LAND COMPANY.

This company was organized in 1893, with a capital of $10,000. It owns fifty-four acres of the most desirable residential property in Rock Hill, situated in the eastern portion of the city and commanding a splendid view of the city and the country around. Its property has been laid off into lots and streets, is now on the market, and lots can be purchased at reasonable rates. This company was a competitor with the Town Site Company for the location of the Normal and Industrial College, and gave its rival a close race for this institution.

Its property is beautifully situated, is undulating and well-drained, and has good water. High-toned and substantial gentlemen are the promoters of this organization, and they take pleasure in showing their properties to visitors to the city.

The Officers are: Iredell Jones, President; Frel Mobley, Vice-President; D. Hutchison, Secretary and Treasurer.

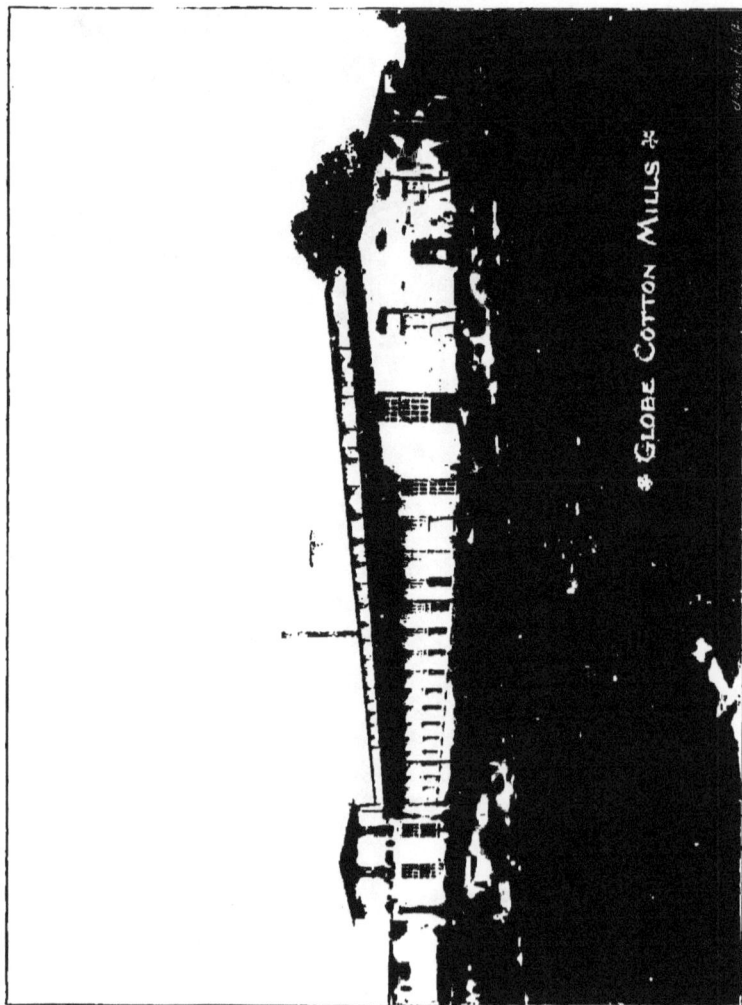

✢ GLOBE COTTON MILLS ✢

## CITY LOTS.

It is but natural that real estate should have advanced in prices in Rock Hill in view of the rapid growth of the place ; but taking into consideration all of the advantages accruing to the citizen residing here, the prices are still quite reasonable. Good residence property in a desirable location, with a depth of from 180 to 200 feet can be purchased at from three to five dollars per front foot; of course, the best residence property sells at a much higher rate. Lots of the same depth in the business portion of the city sell at from $50 to $100 per front foot. There is never a period when the sale of lots is not going on, steadily and oftentimes rapidly, as the city is building up and expanding.

## FARM LANDS.

The farm lands in this section are various in character, and always fertile and productive. To the north and west of Rock Hill the lands have mostly clay and mulatto sub-soils, and their fertility is capable of being greatly increased. These lands are adapted to the raising of cotton, corn, tobacco, wheat, oats, rye, clover and the grasses. To the south and east, the lands are sandy and black-jack. While a few years ago these black-jack lands were regarded as of little value, on account of their liability to produce "rust" on growing cotton, the use of potash has fully redeemed and reclaimed the greater part of them, and they are now regarded as the best farming lands in the country. Some of these black-jack lands produce corn equal to that which grows on the richest alluvial bottoms.

The sandy lands in this section are productive of cotton; and are specially adapted to the raising of tobacco, as is shown elsewhere in this manual.

Little attention has been paid to the cultivation of the grasses here, but large quantities of hay are gathered from the volunteer growth of numerous meadow lands. Stock, cattle and sheep raising has received some attention ; and the raising of hogs has come to be regarded as an indispensable part of farm operations.

# Real Estate Brokerage.

The Rock Hill Real Estate Agency was established in 1894. Prior to this time, such a business as a real estate brokerage was unknown in the city. There were land companies and renting agents, and agents who represented others on a small scale in the sale of real estate; but the brokerage feature was entirely new, and in most cases each individual or company acted for himself or itself in the purchase and sale of real estate.

The time, however, had come for a change; and necessity became the mother of the land brokerage business. Extensive operations in real estate demanded that there must be an intelligence bureau where people could go to learn of it. A live and growing city must have real estate to sell, and there must be some one whose business it is to sell it. It was on this economical principle of a proper distribution of labor that this agency was founded and is succeeding. It serves its patrons as vendor or purchaser; and buys options on real estate when desired. In a word, it is engaged in everything pertaining to the real estate business in all of its ramifications.

This agency is the affair of W. J. Cherry, and is under his sole management.

## HOMES FOR IMMIGRANTS.

The Rock Hill Real Estate Agency is not limited in its operations to the City of Rock Hill, but controls the sale of large quantities of land in York County, and the adjacent Counties of Lancaster and Chester. These lands embrace many distinct tracts, some of which are contiguous to each other, and special inducements are offered to colonies of immigrants who are desirous of settling in the same neighborhood. A large area of fine farming lands in the Waxhaw section of Lancaster County, and along the east bank of the Catawba River, in the Counties of Lancaster and York, can be bought on easy terms at prices ranging from five dollars per acre upwards. These lands are in a healthy section of country, some of them finely timbered, and all conveniently located near the Ohio River and Charleston, and Georgia, Carolina and Northern Railroads. The low prices at which these lands can be bought are due to the sparse population of their locality, and the scarcity of money which has tied up all interests all over the country for the past few years. They would be cheap at double the prices asked, and are certain to enhance in value as population increases and farming interests are improved. They compare favorably in fertility with the best lands in Lancaster County, and are adapted to the growing of cotton, corn, tobacco, wheat, oats, clover and other crops. While some of these lands are in Lancaster County, they are nearer to Rock Hill than to the town of Lancaster, and Rock Hill is the market for produce raised in that vicinity.

Farmers of the Northwest, who have failed on account of adverse conditions, and who desire homes where their labors will be crowned with a proper reward, will do well to turn their footsteps in this direction. The Piedmont Section is sure to become the garden spot of the American Continent, and those who cast their lots here, under these auspicious Southern skies, will bless the day that decided their choice.

Factory sites and valuable water-powers are for sale by this agency, and its manager is always delighted to correspond with manufacturers who desire a location.

### REAL ESTATE.—RENTING.

Col. John J. Waters is the pioneer in this business, and now does the renting and collecting of rents for the city. He is an intelligent, courteous and affable gentleman, and if renting be your business, you cannot do better than to cultivate an acquaintance with him and his properties.

●  ●

# Telephone, Postal and Other Facilities.

The city has a Telephone Company, and a first-class system of telephonic intercommunication is one of its conveniences. It connects all of the business houses, shops, offices, depots and factories, and includes a large number of the private residences. This company has the franchise for connecting with other towns in the County.

Rock Hill has also a long distance telephone connection with Charlotte, Salisbury, Concord and other towns in North Carolina. Its postal, telegraph and express facilities are first-class.

● ●

## fire Department.

Rock Hill has a well-equipped and efficient Fire Department, which is in charge of the young men of the town. Their services are principally voluntary, though certain privileges and exemptions are granted to them. They are sufficiently patriotic to be always counted on, and large pay is not a necessary incentive. There is also a colored fire company, which can be depended on to render effective services at a fire.

The facilities for extinguishing fire are: A Silsby steamer managed by the Rock Hill Steam Fire Company and a hook and ladder truck, controlled by the colored fire company. Large cisterns judiciously located furnish an ample supply of water.

The Silsby is a noble fire extinguisher, and has many times paid for itself in property saved.

● ●

## newspaper.

Rock Hill has one newspaper, the *Herald*, which is published twice a week. The corporation has always had a live paper, which has done its part in building up the city. The *Herald* was established in 1876, by the late James M. Ivy. Mr. J. J. Hull bought the paper in 1886, and has owned it continuously since. Mr. Hull is editor as well as proprietor. Besides being an able writer, he is an experienced and practical printer, and the appearance of his paper bears evidence of his fitness for his calling.

THE ARCADE COTTON MILL — IN COURSE OF ERECTION.

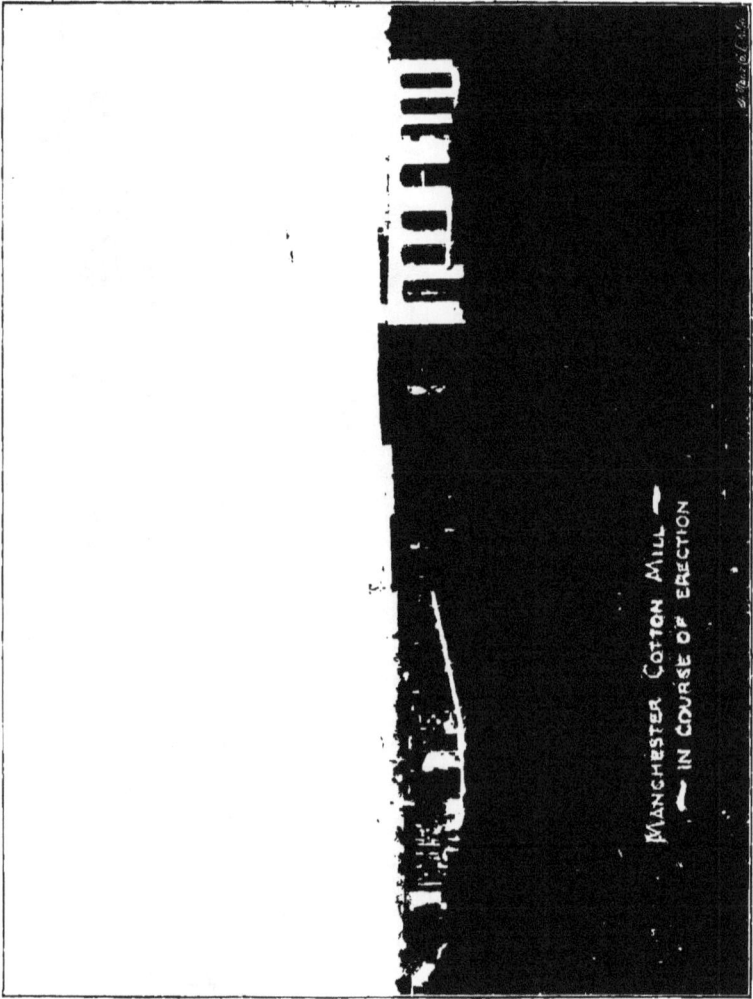

Manchester Cotton Mill — in course of erection

# Public Library.

One of the valued institutions of the city is its Public Library. It is well supplied with books and current literature, and is quite attractive to visitors, who are always welcomed and politely received by the Librarian in charge. It has also been made the depository of the records of the Fifth Congressional District. It is maintained by an association composed of the citizens of the city; and the city government exercises a fostering care, and has provided for its welfare in its organic law.

• •

# Federal Building in Prospect.

The next good thing in store for Rock Hill is most likely a Federal building. There is a movement now being made for the establishment of a United States Court House in this section, and as there is a large amount of mail business at this place, which is daily increasing, it is highly probable that Congress will provide for the erection of a building at Rock Hill, combining a postoffice and court room. A bill has already been introduced in Congress to establish a court house here, and its chances for becoming a law are reported to be favorable.

• •

# Streets.

Rock Hill has now about ten miles of macadamized streets, smooth and in fine condition. Main and Railroad Streets have granite sidewalks, laid with granite obtained from quarries just outside of the corporate limits. The important work of grading and macadamizing the streets, and constructing granite sidewalks, was begun in 1889, in which year town bonds to the amount of $5,000 were issued for the purpose. It was found that this amount would fall far short of what was necessary for the work begun ; and so, in 1891, additional bonds to the amount of $10,000 were issued. With the funds derived from these bonds, a good and substantial work has been done, and Rock Hill now has first-class streets that will be as enduring as the city itself.

The following gentlemen composed the Council under which this important work was begun, and to them is largely due the credit for its accomplishment: J. M. Cherry, Intendant; R. T. Fewell, A. D. Holler, J. J. Hagins and D. C. Williams, Wardens.

● ●

## Macadamized Roads.

Good roads in a community are as important as good streets in a town or city; and, other things being equal, that town or city which has smooth, substantial highways leading into it will far outstrip the one which is difficult to reach because of rough and neglected roads. The facilities being alike, people will go to do their marketing to the place which is easiest of access. The saving from properly constructed roads is not only one of comfort and convenience, but also one of dollars and cents; for no argument is needed to show that vehicles will last longest and horses will have to be shod the least number of times where the roads are the best. All of these matters have been considered in Rock Hill, and she is solving the question of good country highways for herself. If her sister cities and towns in the State would follow her example in this respect, the road question would be solved in South Carolina. If all the municipal corporations in the State would build good roads from their limits as far into the country as their resources would permit, the people in the country would soon emulate their example in extending the work, and there would soon be no bad roads in the State.

The plan of macadamizing the roads around Rock Hill was conceived by Dr. T. A. Crawford, a prominent citizen of the city, and its successful execution is the result of his efficient head work and unconquerable energy.

In the Spring of 1891, Dr. Crawford proposed to the corporate authorities that if they would macadamize Elm Avenue to the city limits, and contribute one-fourth of the cost of extending it for a distance of two miles beyond, he would undertake to procure the people in the country who used the road, to contribute the other three-fourths of the expenses. The Council accepted the proposition and, with this as a lever, Dr. Crawford succeeded in getting the people of the neighborhood using the road to undertake their part of the work. Subscriptions were permitted to be paid in labor and by the use of wagons and teams, and for every three dollars thus subscribed the City Council subscribed and paid one dollar. The County Commissioners were induced to have stumps and rocks removed, and to furnish an engine and rock crusher.

The road, thirty feet wide, was laid off by a civil engineer, and the water-ways marked. The surface of the road-way was then made loose by ploughing, and the earth was thrown to the middle of the road with a street plough, making it twelve inches higher in the middle than at the sides. It was then rolled with a two ton iron roller, and the crushed rock laid on to a depth of from five to eight inches and covering a width of nine feet. The rock was then rolled by the same roller and packed. This was the complete process; and a road leading through marshy lands, which sometimes through the winter months could scarcely be travelled, was thus transformed into one of the finest roads in the country, and is now become a favorite drive-way for inhabitants of the city. It is a lasting memorial of the progressiveness of a worthy citizen, and in his honor it bears the name of the "Crawford Road."

This road enters Rock Hill from the South. It was such a successful experiment that another road was built on the same plan three miles long, entering Rock Hill from the Southeast. The entire cost of the two roads was about $3,000; so that the city has only expended about $750 in the work.

Other Rock Hill roads are soon to receive similar treatment, and Rock Hill is thus gradually becoming the center of a ststem of first-class roads.

# How the City is Lighted.

The city has an efficient system of electric lighting, embracing arc lights for the streets and incandescent for buildings and residences. The plant is the property of a private corporation, which was organized in 1890, by residents of the city. This company has a contract with the city for lighting the streets, embracing a period of six years, and by which it is permitted to light residences and to furnish lights for all private purposes. The plant is conveniently located for its purpose, and electricity is generated by two engines aggregating two hundred and twenty-five horse-power.

This company now lights most of the residences of the city, furnishes lights for the Rock Hill Cotton Factory, and does the lighting for the Winthrop Normal College.

J. M. Cherry is President of the company. The Directors are: J. M. Cherry, Jno. R. London, D. Hutchison, A. H. White, Julius Friedheim, J. F. Reid and R. T. Fewell.

● ●

# Business.

Respecting the business character and prospects of this "hustling" little city, it is scarcely necessary to speak, when the facts and figures already stated have been considered. It would be solecistic to write about a "loafer" in Rock Hill. Such an anomalous creature is an impossibility in this atmosphere. A loafer would be so solitary here that he would languish and die of ennui; or else he would be hatched from his chrysalis state into a useful, active and busy citizen. The men of business are intelligent, industrious men of affairs, who do not underrate the dignity of labor. They have always realized that they must work for the "daily bread" for which they pray. In this way, they have acquired an enviable reputation for business ability, and have built up for themselves a large and valuable trade. While the city is self-sustaining and can live on her own resources, she has always been in touch with the country around; and she draws trade from all parts of York County, and from adjacent counties.

44

FACTORY OF

The secret of the wonderful success of this granite city of the hills is to be found in the fact that she has always steered straight between the Scylla of dissension and the Charybdis of unbelief in the possibilities of her future. Faith and Unity are the magic words emblazoned on her escutcheon; and she believes in no talisman except Pluck. Her history from the beginning is aptly summarized as "a long pull, a strong pull, and a pull all together."

• •

## Taxation, Indebtedness and Resources.

Among the first inquiries some persons will make about a place are questions about taxation and indebtedness. In fact, there are some persons who seem to have a constitutional horror for taxes and bonded indebtedness. Such persons are properly classified as "moss-backs," and they usually live in some little shriveled up municipality where the wheels of progress are hopelessly clogged. Fortunately for Rock Hill, the genus has never appeared.

The citizens of Rock Hill are neither parsimonious nor extravagant; but they have not hesitated to go in debt for a good thing that is offered, if convinced that it is a prudent thing to do, in view of all the circumstances. In this way the city has climbed to her vantage-ground. Property has increased in amount and value as different issues in bonds have been made, so that the raise in taxes has been scarcely appreciable. The bonded debt of $86,000, compared with property and resources, is reasonable, and eight and a half mills, the rate of taxation is actually small in comparison with the rate in our most populous and wealthy cities. So Rock Hill's taxes are reasonable, she does not owe more than she can easily pay at maturity; and back of it all, she has a brainy, plucky and tireless people as part of her available resources.

• •

## Biographical.

Some interesting biographies could be picked up in Rock Hill, and it would doubtless be instructive to study the individual histories and characters of the men who are engaged in building the city now receiving the attention of the writer; but such an idea is foreign to the purpose of this little book, and it is preferred for those who have the inclination and the patience to read these pages to gather their ideas of the individual citizens of Rock Hill from the deeds they have done, and which are here set down. In this way, a sufficiently clear idea of *who* and *what* the men are will be obtained.

• •

# final.

The conclusion of the story of Rock Hill brings the writer back to the beginning, and makes him feel like qualifying what was there said by asking to make some explanations.

He realizes the many imperfections in the task which was undertaken. It is illogical in arrangement, the subject-matter being set down as it occurred to the writer, without regard to the relation of the different topics. The apology for this is, that it had to be written hastily amid the pressing demands of other duties; the writer had no model for his work before him; and he had consequently to write thus at random. There are doubtless important matters overlooked which should have received attention ; on the other hand, in undertaking a pen picture of Rock Hill (the home of the writer) he has had to avoid falling into the error of an unworthy attempt at flourishes. He has striven to give a faithful portrayal, and is conscientious in believing that he has stated the truth in all that is written ; and if there are any doubting Thomases into whose hands these lines may come, they are asked to come to Rock Hill and "prove the pudding" for themselves.

It is not claimed that Rock Hill has all that an ambitious city could desire, and that she is altogether self-satisfied. Such a claim would involve nothing but reproach. Much more is desired for her. Good, honest and deserving men and women are invited to come and make Rock Hill their home. Capital is desired, and is invited, with the assurance beforehand that there will always be satisfactory profits for the investor in Rock Hill enterprises. A welcome is here for honest brawn and brain in all of the departments of human activity. Parents with children to educate are asked to come and enjoy the splendid advantages here given. The latch string is on the outside to all who have an honest purpose in life, and are trying to measure up to the great responsibilities of living. All such are invited to come to Rock Hill and cast their lots in a live and growing city which is marching with magical swiftness to a glorious destiny in the New South.

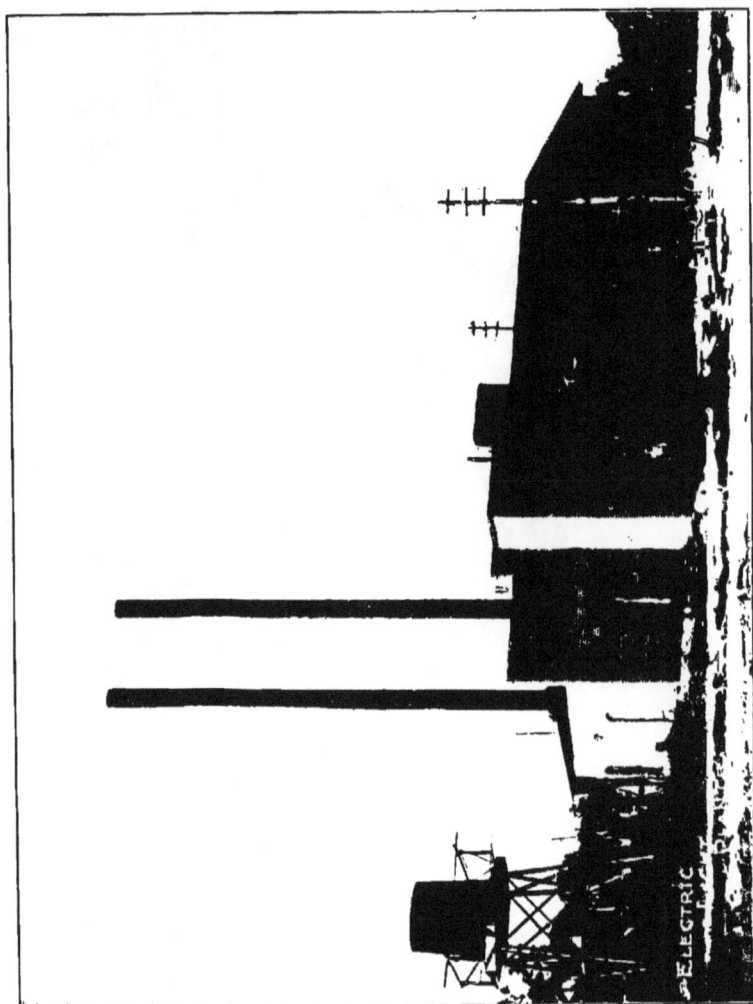

# Directory.

**General Mercantile Business**—Roddey Mercantile Co., Main Street; A. Friedheim & Bro., Main Street; R. T. Fewell & Co., Main Street and Railroad Avenue; A. E. Smith & Co., Main Street; C. W. Frew, Main Street; J. W. O'Neal, corner Main Street and Railroad Avenue.

**Family Groceries**—L. M. Davis, Railroad Avenue; W. Oakman, Railroad Avenue; Bryant & Avery, Main Street; J. N. McElwee & Co., Main Street; J. J. Hagins & Co., Railroad Avenue; Ausband Bros., (also sell furniture,) corner Main and Church Streets; W. J. Caveny, Main Street; W. S. Nicholson, Main Street.

**Dry Goods, Clothing, Shoes**—August Friedheim, Main Street; S. Segal, Railroad Avenue.

**Racket Stores**—New York Racket, True & Klutz, Proprietors, Main Street; The Robertson Company, Main Street.

**Vehicles**—Rock Hill Buggy Co., Wilson Street; Reid & Wroton, Main Street.

**Furniture, Stoves, Undertaking**—S. T. Frew & Co., Main Street; Reid & Wroton, Main Street.

**Druggists**—J. B. Johnson & Co., Main Street; M. H. Sandifer, Main Street; A. J. Evans, Main Street; J. J. Hagins & Co., Railroad Avenue.

**Cotton Firms**—A. E. Smith & Co.; R. T. Fewell & Co.; A. Friedheim & Bro.; Ed. Fewell; Ruff & Morrison; Heath, Springs & Co., represented by T. L. Johnson; Sanders, Orr & Co., represented by Zeb. Johnson.

**Machine Shops and Foundry**—W. S. Creighton & Co., office in factory building, near Main Street.

**Jewelers**—George Beach, Main Street; I. Blumberg, Main Street.

**Millinery and Mantua Making**—Ratterree & Adams, millinery; Misses Erwin & Proctor, mantua makers; Miss Mary Smith, mantua maker; Mrs. Tuggle, mantua maker; Roddey Mercantile Co., millinery; R. T. Fewell & Co., millinery.

**Hardware**—Rock Hill Hardware Co., Main Street.

**Meat Market**—V. B. McFadden, Main Street; Kerr & Peacock, corner Main and Hampton Streets; John Mallard, corner Main and Wilson Streets.

**Livery and Sale Stables**—Kerr & Heath, West Main Street; J. W. Marshall, Hampton Street; J. Harvey Neely, corner Main and Church Streets.

**Saddles and Harness**—McFadden & Johnson, Main Street.

**Brokers**—B. N. Craig, merchandise broker and commission merchant, Main Street; W. A. Fewell, merchandise broker and commission merchant, Library Building; Watts & Wood, cotton, stock and bond brokers (private leased wire connections with New York, New Orleans and Chicago,) Main Street; J. D. Scruggs, merchandise broker and commission merchant.

**Railroad and Express Companies**—J. E. Forney, local passenger and freight agent of the Southern Railway Co., and of the Southern Express Co., offices in depots of Southern Railway Co.; A. C. Izard, soliciting freight agent of the Southern Railway Co. T. B. Lumpkin, local agent of the Ohio River and Charleston Railway Co., offices at O. R. & C. Railway depot.

**Life and Fire Insurance**—Representatives: W. J. Roddey, D. Hutchison, L. Sherfesee, P. C. Poag, Jno. R. London.

**Western Union Telegraph Company**—Office: Library building, Main Street.

**Banks**—First Fational, W. L. Roddey, President; W. J. Roddey, Vice-President; J. H. Miller, Cashier; R. Lee Kerr, Teller; L. C. Harrison, Bookkeeper. Savings Bank, D. Hutchison, President; John R. London, Vice-President; J. M. Cherry, Cashier; Paul Workman, Teller; J. R. Boulware, Bookkeeper.

**Professional**—Ministers: H. R. Moseley, Baptist; H. B. Browne, Methodist; J. W. C. Johnson, Episcopal; Alexander Sprunt, Presbyterian; O. G. Jones, Second Presbyterian; G. T. Harmon, Methodist Presiding Elder, Rock Hill District. Lawyers: W. B. Wilson, J. J. Waters, J. E. Fairey, W. J. Cherry. Physicians: T. A. Crawford, W. F. Strait, T. L. Cornwell, W. J. White, J. M. Hunter, J. A. Meldau, J. P. Crawford, J. E. Massey, J. W. Prather. Dentists: I. Simpson & Son, W. A. Pressley.

**United States Commissioner**—Cad. J. Pride.

**Trial Justice**—J. J. Waters.

**Photographers**—Morley Brothers.

**Librarian**—Miss Lilian Jones.

**City Clerk and Treasurer**—J. D. Scruggs.

**Postmaster**—Cad. J. Pride.

**Carolina Hotel**—A. H. Greene, Proprietor.

**Restaurant**—J. N. McElwee & Co.

**Barber**—J. H. Toole.

LAUREL WOOD * * CEMETERY